From Grain to Pita

Contents

Written by Lorain Day

1

A Staple Food

A staple food is one that people use as a basic part of their diet. People should eat healthy food to keep their bodies healthy and give them energy to grow. Grains are a staple food that should be part of every diet.

Grains are the seeds of grasses that you can eat. There are many types of grains that can be eaten. Grains are an important food for people and for animals.

Grains are produced by grasses.

People all around the world eat grains in many different ways. Some grains are cooked and eaten whole. Some grains are crushed, mixed with milk or water, and cooked. Some grains are dried and toasted.

When the grains are dried and ground into a smooth powder, they become flour. Flour is used to make breads, cakes, cookies, muffins, pastries, and pasta.

When grains are dried and ground into a powder, they become flour or meal.

Some Ways Grains Are Used in Different Places

Place	Grain	Dish
Africa	millet maize (corn)	porridge porridge
America	wheat corn oats	white and brown bread cornbread popcorn breakfast cereals
Australia	wheat	damper
China	rice wheat	steamed rice steamed buns noodles noodles

Place	Grain	Dish
France	wheat	croissants baguettes brioche
Germany	rye	dark, heavy breads
Italy	wheat	pasta focaccia
Mexico	wheat maize (corn)	tortilla tortilla
Middle East	wheat	pita bread
Scotland	oats	oatmeal porridge oatcakes

Grasses You Can Eat

The most common grains people eat belong to the grass family. Thousands of years ago, people ate the seeds from wild grasses. Then they learned to plant the seeds themselves and grow their own crops of grain. This was the beginning of farming.

Common grains belong to the grass family.

People learned that if they saved the seeds from the best plants, they would improve their crops for the next year. As people did this for thousands of years, plants gave better and bigger seeds.

The crops that are grown today look very different from the first ones that were planted. They produce much more grain than the same type of plants did years and years ago.

Today's grain crops look different
from the first ones that were planted.

What Grain Needs to Grow

Aim

If you want to find out what grain needs to grow, you could do an experiment like this.

Materials

- Dried seed corn
- Potting mix
- Refrigerator
- Six small plastic pots or cartons
- Two small boxes
- Water

Method

1 Put potting mix into the plant pots. Number the pots from 1 to 6. Push one corn seed into the middle of each pot. Cover it with soil. Label each pot with its number and the date. Add enough water to moisten the potting mix in each pot.

2 Put pot 1, pot 2, and pot 3 into one of the small boxes. Put the lid on the box, then put the box into the refrigerator.

3 Put pot 4, pot 5, and pot 6 in the other box. Put the lid on the box. Put the box in a warm place.

4 Every second day, check the pots. If the soil is dry, moisten it with water, but do not add too much.

5 After one week, check each pot. Make notes about what can be seen in each pot.

6 After two weeks, check each pot. Describe what can be seen at the top of the pot. If any seedlings have appeared, measure them and write the results.

7 After three weeks, check each pot. Measure any seedlings that are growing above the soil. Write down the results.

Questions to Consider

Think about what happened.

- Which corn seeds germinated?

- Which corn seeds grew the most?

- Did the corn seeds that germinated have light?

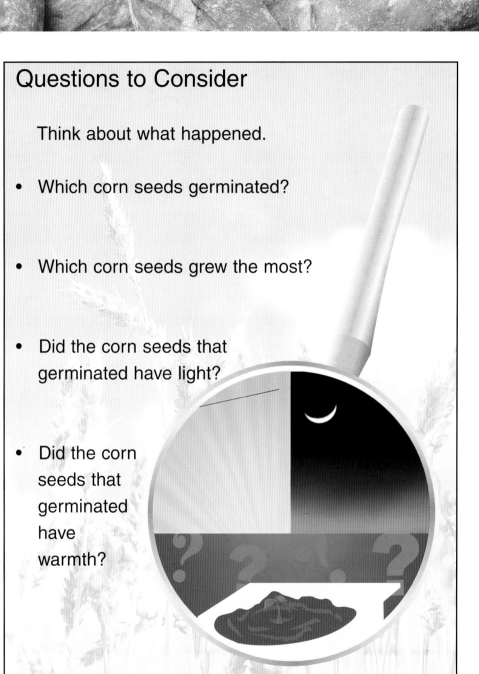

- Did the corn seeds that germinated have warmth?

Has the question at the beginning of the experiment been answered? Check your notes.

Day 2 - watered pots

Day 4 - watered pots

End of week 1 - nothing showing in pots 1, 2, and 3. Pots 4, 5, and 6 have nothing showing. Watered pots.

End of week 2 - pots 1, 2, and 3 have nothing showing. Pots 4 and 5, in a warm place, have shoots showing. Watered pots.

End of week 3 - still nothing in pots 1, 2, and 3. Pots 4 and 5 have big shoots and some leaves. Pot 6 has a shoot, too.

Notes and information could be recorded in a chart like this.

Corn-seed Record					
Environment			Growth		
Pot	Water	Warmth	Week 1	Week 2	Week 3
1	✓	✗	✗	✗	✗
2	✓	✗	✗	✗	✗
3	✓	✗	✗	✗	✗
4	✓	✓	✗	✓	✓
5	✓	✓	✗	✓	✓
6	✓	✓	✗	✗	✓
✗ no			✓ yes		

The History of Bread

People have been making bread for thousands of years. Early cave people crushed the seeds of wild grasses between rocks. This made rough flour. They mixed the flour with water to make dough.

Then the cave people made thin, hard bread by cooking the dough on flat rocks they had heated in a fire.

People have made bread
for thousands of years.

The people of Ancient Egypt learned how to make their bread softer by adding yeast and honey to the dough. The yeast reacted with the sugar in the honey, and made tiny bubbles of gas that made the bread rise. When the bread cooked, it became much bigger and lighter, and was softer and sweeter to eat. Bread that rises is leavened bread. Bread that does not rise is unleavened bread, or flat bread.

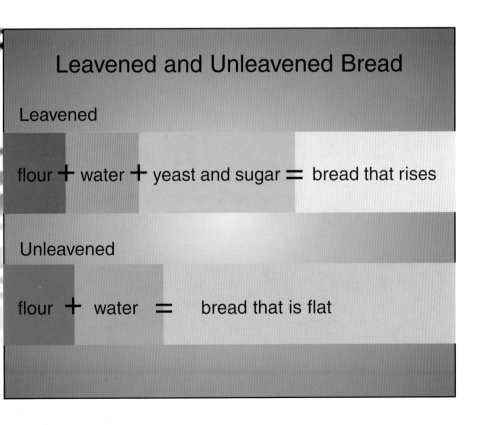

Leavened and Unleavened Bread

Leavened

flour + water + yeast and sugar = bread that rises

Unleavened

flour + water = bread that is flat

Grain Used for Different Types of Bread

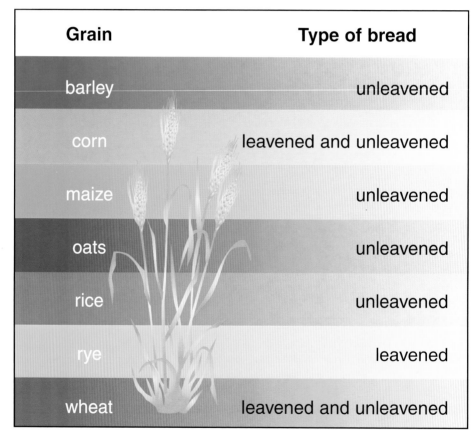

Grain	Type of bread
barley	unleavened
corn	leavened and unleavened
maize	unleavened
oats	unleavened
rice	unleavened
rye	leavened
wheat	leavened and unleavened

The Greeks and Romans learned how to make leavened bread from the Egyptians. When the Romans ruled most of Europe, they taught the local people how to make leavened bread, too.

Many people learned how to make leavened bread.

Since the Middle Ages, most of the people in Europe have known how to make leavened bread. There were flour mills that ground flour and bakeries that baked and sold bread.

In the past, bakeries made and sold bread. They still do today.

People either made their own bread at home or bought it from bakeries. Most people who lived in rural areas and on farms made their own bread.

Some people made their own bread at home.

When the wheat was ground at the mill, the miller could make two kinds of flour. If the miller left the husks in the flour, it was brown flour, or whole-wheat flour. This was what most people used to bake dark heavy breads. It was the cheapest flour.

Whole-wheat flour makes dark heavy bread.

If the miller separated the husks from the flour, it was sold as fine white flour and was made into white bread. Because separating the husks was extra work, white flour was more expensive. Only wealthy people could afford to eat white bread.

White flour makes white bread.

When it became easier and cheaper to make white flour, white bread became one of the most common foods in Europe and North America.

White bread is a common food.

Today, most people eat bread that is made in a factory or bakery and sold in a supermarket, but many people still like to make their own bread as well.

People still like to make their own bread.

Wheat: From Field to Table

1 Grain is produced on grasses that grow from seeds. Grasses grow until the adult plant is covered with new seeds.

6 The dough is baked to make bread. Different ways of baking make different kinds of bread.

5 The flour is mixed with water and other ingredients to make dough. Different ingredients make different kinds of bread.

2 When the plant is fully grown, it dries out and turns golden. It is then harvested.

3 A harvesting machine separates the seeds from the stalks. This is called threshing and winnowing.

4 The seeds are dried more before they are ground into flour.

Making Damper

Damper is a bread that is cooked over a fire using a stick. If you are camping, damper is a good bread to make.

What You Will Need to Make Damper

- One tablespoon of butter or vegetable shortening
- Two cups of flour
- Two teaspoons of baking powder
- One-quarter teaspoon of salt
- One cup of milk

- Bowl
- Clean board or flat surface
- Knife
- Measuring cup
- Strong clean stick
- Tablespoon
- Teaspoon

How to Make Damper

1 Measure the flour and put it into the bowl. Measure the salt and mix it into the flour.

2 Use the knife to cut the butter, or shortening, into small pieces. Put the pieces into the bowl with the flour and salt.

3 Using your fingers, rub the flour mixture and the pieces of butter, or shortening, until they look like crumbs. There should not be any lumps in the mixture.

4 Make a hole in the middle of the mixture. Pour in most of the milk, but save about a quarter of a cup.

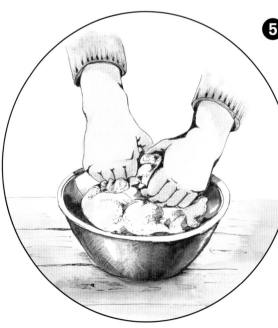

5 Stir the milk into the mixture. When it gets too difficult to stir with the spoon, use your hands. Quickly mix all the flour into the dough you are making. Do not leave any of the flour on the sides of the bowl.

6 When you have made a soft dough, put some flour onto the clean board. Put the dough onto the floured board.

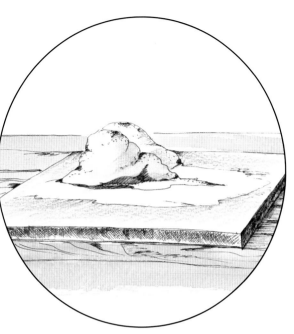

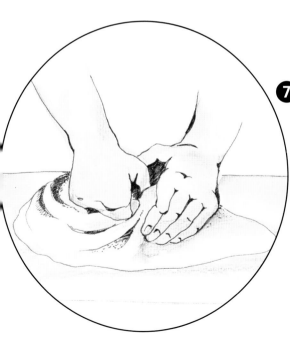

7 Rub any leftover dough from your hands, then dip them in some flour. Use your hands to knead the dough for about two minutes.

How to Knead

Hold the dough on the board gently with one hand.

Use the heel of your other hand (the part below your thumb) to push the dough away from you.

Fold the side you have pushed away back onto the ball of dough and push it in.

Now do the same thing again, but this time hold the side that you pushed before, and push away the other side.

Then turn the ball of dough over and around.

Sprinkle the dough with some flour so it doesn't stick to the board.

Keep doing these steps until the dough is smooth and not sticky.

8 Roll the dough into a long thick sausage shape. Wind the dough around and along the stick. Press it firmly to the stick so it will not fall off. Brush the rest of the milk over the dough on the stick.

9 Cook the damper over the hot coals of a campfire, turning it so that it cooks evenly on all sides. Hold the stick as if you were toasting marshmallows. The damper should be cooked in 5 to 10 minutes. It should be golden brown.

Glossary

crops – Plants grown on a large scale, usually for food.

diet – The types of food a person or community usually eats.

dough – A thick mixture of flour, liquid, and other ingredients used to make bread or pastry.

husks – The dry outside parts of seeds, which can be removed.

mill(s) – A place where grain is ground into flour. The machinery itself is also called a mill.

miller – A person who works in a mill.

seedlings – Small plants that have grown from seeds.

yeast – A type of fungus used for fermenting, and to make bread rise.